First World War
and Army of Occupation
War Diary
France, Belgium and Germany

58 DIVISION
Divisional Troops
Divisional Ammunition Column
6 January 1917 - 31 May 1919

WO95/2995/7

The Naval & Military Press Ltd
www.nmarchive.com
Published in association with The National Archives

Published by

The Naval & Military Press Ltd

Unit 10 Ridgewood Industrial Park,

Uckfield, East Sussex,

TN22 5QE England

Tel: +44 (0) 1825 749494

www.naval-military-press.com

www.nmarchive.com

This diary has been reprinted in facsimile from the original. Any imperfections are inevitably reproduced and the quality may fall short of modern type and cartographic standards.

© **Crown Copyright**
Images reproduced by permission of The National Archives, London, England, 2015.

Contents

Document type	Place/Title	Date From	Date To
Heading	WO95/2995-6		
Heading	58th Divl Ammn Column Jan 1917-1919 May		
War Diary	Winchester	06/01/1917	06/01/1917
War Diary	Southampton	26/01/1917	27/01/1917
War Diary	Harve	28/01/1917	29/01/1917
Heading	War Diary 58th D.A.C. From 1-1-17 To 31-1-17 Vol. 1		
War Diary	Southampton	03/02/1917	03/02/1917
War Diary	Harve	04/02/1917	04/02/1917
War Diary	Southampton	04/02/1917	04/02/1917
War Diary	Harve	05/02/1917	05/02/1917
War Diary	Southampton	05/02/1917	05/02/1917
War Diary	Mezerolles	06/02/1917	06/02/1917
War Diary	Harve	06/02/1917	06/02/1917
War Diary	Mezerolles	07/02/1917	07/02/1917
War Diary	Harve	07/02/1917	07/02/1917
War Diary	Mezerolles	08/02/1917	24/02/1917
War Diary	Warlicourt	24/02/1917	24/02/1917
War Diary	La Bezeque	24/02/1917	24/02/1917
War Diary	Grouches	24/02/1917	24/02/1917
War Diary	Warlicourt	25/02/1917	25/02/1917
War Diary	La Bezeque	27/02/1917	28/02/1917
Heading	War Diary 58th D.A.C. From 1-2-17 To 28-2-17 Volume 2		
War Diary	Mezerolles	01/02/1918	28/02/1918
Heading	War Diary 58th D.A.C. From 1-2-17 To 28-2-17 Vol. II.		
War Diary	Warlincourt	01/03/1917	26/03/1917
War Diary	Bienvillers	15/04/1917	15/04/1917
War Diary	Ervillers	15/04/1917	15/04/1917
Heading	War Diary Of 58th D.A.C. From 1/5/17 To 28/5/17		
War Diary	In The Field		
War Diary	In The Field	04/07/1917	07/09/1917
War Diary	Vlamertinghe	02/11/1917	02/11/1917
War Diary	Wormhoudt	03/11/1917	03/11/1917
War Diary	Ruminghem	12/11/1917	12/11/1917
War Diary	Desvres	13/11/1917	13/11/1917
War Diary	Tubersent	14/11/1917	14/11/1917
War Diary	Frencq	18/11/1917	18/11/1917
War Diary	Maresville	04/12/1917	04/12/1917
War Diary	Merck-St-Lievin	05/12/1917	05/12/1917
War Diary	Lederzeele	06/12/1917	06/12/1917
War Diary	Zermezeele	07/12/1917	31/01/1918
War Diary	Baboeuf	06/02/1918	06/02/1918
War Diary		22/03/1918	27/03/1918
Heading	58th Divisional Ammunition Column. April 1918		
War Diary		01/04/1918	11/04/1918
War Diary			
War Diary	Eaucourt Sur Somme	06/05/1918	06/05/1918
War Diary	Bourdon	07/05/1918	07/05/1918
War Diary	Eaucourt Sur Somme	16/05/1918	16/05/1918

War Diary	Belloy	17/05/1918	17/05/1918
War Diary	Contay	24/05/1918	09/06/1918
War Diary	B.9.c	10/06/1918	10/06/1918
War Diary	Longpre	19/06/1918	19/06/1918
War Diary	Picquigny	20/06/1918	30/06/1918
Heading	58th Divisional Ammunition Column. August 1918.		
War Diary	Near Contay	03/08/1918	03/08/1918
War Diary	Behencourt	08/08/1918	08/08/1918
War Diary	La Neuville	09/08/1918	09/08/1918
War Diary	Bonnay	12/08/1918	12/08/1918
War Diary	Sailly-Le-Sec	27/08/1918	27/08/1918
War Diary	Meaulte	28/08/1918	28/08/1918
War Diary	Etinehem	30/08/1918	31/08/1918
War Diary	Nr Maricourt	05/09/1918	05/09/1918
War Diary	Clery. S. Somme	06/09/1918	06/09/1918
War Diary	Allaines	09/09/1918	30/09/1918
War Diary	Nr Moislains	08/10/1918	08/10/1918
War Diary	Nr Bony	09/10/1918	09/10/1918
War Diary	Nr. Driencourt	11/10/1918	12/10/1918
War Diary	Bully Grenay	13/10/1918	13/10/1918
War Diary	Moroc	13/10/1918	13/10/1918
War Diary	Hersin	18/10/1918	18/10/1918
War Diary	Montigny	19/10/1918	19/10/1918
War Diary	Evin	20/10/1918	20/10/1918
War Diary	La Vacquerie	21/10/1918	21/10/1918
War Diary	Lannay	09/11/1918	09/11/1918
War Diary	Nr Rongy	10/11/1918	10/11/1918
War Diary	Le Croix	11/11/1918	11/11/1918
War Diary	Stambruges	12/11/1918	12/11/1918
War Diary	Grand Glise	11/12/1918	11/12/1918
War Diary	Beloeil	01/05/1919	31/05/1919

WO 95/2995/6

58TH DIVISION

58TH DIVL AMMN COLUMN

JAN 1917 — ~~DEC 191~~ 1917 MAR

Box 2995

Army Form C. 2118.

WAR DIARY of 38th J.B.A.C.

INTELLIGENCE SUMMARY

(Erase heading not required.)

January 1917.

Vol 1

Place	Date	Hour	Summary of Events and Information	Remarks and references to Appendices
WINCHESTER	JAN. 6		Received final orders to mobilize.	
SOUTHAMPTON	26	7.10 pm	H.Q. and Nº1 Section Embarked. See below —	
	27	9¾am	H.Q. and Nº1 Section arrived at HARVE.	
	28	10pm	H.Q. and Nº1 Section left HARVE.	
HARVE	29	9½am	H.Q. and Nº1 Section Troops arrived MEZEROLLES	
			※ A, delay in embarkation now took place, owing to Confusion at HARVE.	

J.B.W.Evans
Lieut. Col. R.F.A.,
Commanding 58th (L.C.

War Diary
58th D.A.C.
From 1-1-17. To 31-1-17.
Vol. 1

AF C 2118

Sheet 1.

WAR DIARY of 50th D.A.C.
February 1917.

Vol 2

Place	Date	Hour	Summary of Events and Information	Remarks & References to Appendices
SOUTHAMPTON	3rd	7.15pm	No 1 Section embarked at SOUTHAMPTON.	
HARVE	4th	6½am	No 1 Section arrived HARVÉ	
SOUTHAMPTON	"	7.15pm	No 3 Section embarked at SOUTHAMPTON	
HARVE.	5	Midnight	No 3 Section arrived HARVÉ	
"	"	8½pm 9½am	No 2 Section left HARVE	
SOUTHAMPTON	"	7.30 pm	No 4 Section embarked at SOUTHAMPTON	
HEZEROULES	6.	4.30pm	No 2 Section arrived HEZEROULES	
HARVE	"	7½pm	No 3 Section left HARVÉ.	
"	"	9½am	No 4 Section arrived HARVÉ	
HEZEROULES	7.	5.30am	No 3 Section arrived HEZEROULES	
HARVE	"	7.30am	No 4 Section left HARVÉ — 1 Officer 7 other Ranks 30 L.D. Horses joined from D/293 Batteries	
HEZEROULES	8	7½pm	No 4 Section both arrived HEZEROULES	
"	9th	2½pm	No 4 Section left HEZEROULES and then camped at OUTREBOIS	
"	11th		D.A.C. reorganised i.e. H.Q. "A" Echelon 2 Sections and "B" Echelon – Strength:- Officers 15 Other Ranks 696 Ride Horses 76 L.D. 816 Total 892	
"			293 A.F.A. B.A.C. formed — Strength Officers 3 Other Ranks 147 Ride Horses 21 L.D. 170 Total 191.	
"	16th		50 G.S. wagons and 50 pr Horses attached to 49th D.A.C.	

Army Form C2118
Sheet 1.

WAR DIARY of 58th D.A.C.
February 1917.

PLACE	DATE	HOUR	SUMMARY OF EVENTS AND INFORMATION	Remarks and reference to appendices
MEZEROLLES	18th		New Designation of Sections in accordance with reorganization. 28 Wagons G.S. & Teams T/b attached to Divisional Train. No 3 Section becomes No 1. No 2 Section No change. No 4 Section becomes No 3 Section "B" Relay.	
"	19th		11 Other Ranks left on posting to Trench Mortar Batteries.	
"	20th		9 Reinforcements arrived from Trench Mortar Batteries.	
"	21st		5 Other Ranks left for duty at Divisional Baths at P.A.S.	
"	22nd		12 horses sent to Base Hospital and struck off Strength.	
"	23rd		4 Reinforcements arrived from Trench Mortar Batteries. Lieut A.H. Soutsby assumed command of Amn Section vice Capt W.I. LINDSAY for B.E.S. proc'd to Command 293rd A.F.A. B.Q.C. 78 G.S. wagons returned from 58th Div Train and T9th D.A.C.	
"	24th		D.A.C. moved from MEZEROLLES and OUTRE BOIS	
WARLICOURT			H.Q. arrived and encamped at WARLICOURT.	
LA BEZEGUE GROUCHES			No 1 & 2 Sections arrived and encamped at L.A. BEZEGUE FARM. No 3 Sections + 293rd A.F.A. B.A.C. arrived and billetted) for the night at GROUCHES.	
WARLICOURT	25th		No 3 Section arrived and encamped at WARLICOURT.	
LA BEZEQUE	27th		Nos 1+2 Sections moved to P.A.S. and encamped.	
	28th		293rd A.F.A. B.A.C. ceased to be under attached to D.A.C.	

War Diary
58th D.A.C.
from 6.
1-2-17. 28-2-17.
Volume 2.

Army Form C 2118

WAR DIARY of 58(D) D.A.C.
Sketch III
February 1917.

Summary of Events and Information

PLACE	Date	Hour	Summary of Events and Information	Remarks & references to Appendices
MEZEROLLES	1-18.		**Weather** Cold with frosts & snow. Roads in good condition. Variable with rain. A thaw took place rendering the roads in a very bad state. Owing to the bad state of the roads, Mechanical transport was stopped running, consequently a great deal of extra transport had to be done by the D.A.C. and a number of horses had to be evacuated. Consequent upon the bad state of the roads. (i) **Locality** MEZEROLLES. The whole area here is undulating and well watered.	
	18 & 8		**WARLICOURT.** The whole area here is undulating, wooded and, fairly good water supply. (ii) **Roads** All except the Main ARRAS Road are in very bad condition	

J.T.W......... Lieut. Col. R.F.A.
Commanding 58th (Lon.) D.A.C.

WAR DIARY.
58th D.A.C.

From. To.
1-1-17 28-2-17

Vol II

A.F. C2118

WAR DIARY of 58th D.A.C.
March 1917
Vol 3

Sheet 1.

Place	Date	Hour	Summary of Events and Information	Remarks & References to appendices
WARLICOURT.	1st		3 Officers and 22 Other Ranks proceeded to III Army School of Mortars LISNY ST. FOECHAL — 18 Drivers, 36 Horses, 6 wagons attached to 507 By R.E. Weather:— Cold with frost at night — Roads in a very bad state.	
	2nd		1 Horse destroyed. Weather:— Dry and cold, frost at night.	
	3rd		4 reinforcements (Gunners) arrived. 100 Animals clipped. 2/Lieuts. C.H. Strachford and A.L. primrose Stevens joined. H.Q. R.A. moved to BAVICOURT. Weather:— Cold, some snow.	
	4th		1 NCO attached III Army Physical Training Course. Weather:— Cold, frost at night.	
	5th		2 Drivers & Horses attached to Trench Mortar By for ration duty. 1 NCO, 18 Drivers, and 36 horses attached 511 Coy. R.E. Weather:— mild, a light thaw, roads very bad.	
	6th		2 Horses evacuated to M.V.S. Weather:— Mild, thaw continues rendering roads very bad. It is noticed that owing to the bad state of the roads the tires are falling off considerably in consequence.	
	9th		3 Officers and 22 other Ranks returned from Trench mortar Course. 2 Horses evacuated to M.V.S. ability 1 Mule shot. Weather:— Rain and some snow, slight frost at night.	

A.F. C2118

WAR DIARY of 58th D.A.C.
MARCH 1917.

Place	Date	Hour	Summary of Events and Information	Remarks & references to appendices
WAITINGHAM	10th		2 N.C.O.s, 15 Gunners and 5 Drivers posted to Trench Mortar Bty. Weather:- mild with some rain — Roads very badly cut up.	
	11th		400 animals inspected by Brig. Gen. FASSON.	
	12th		2/Lieuts. J.L.Myers and R. Grant joined. 14 Reinforcements (2 NCOs - 8 Gnrs + 4 Drvrs) arrived. Weather:- mild.	
	13th		2/Lieut F.R.Brown attended Sanitary Course M.T.Dz.	
	14th		2/Lieut J.L.Myers posted to 290th Bde R.F.A. 2/Lieut S.R.Boldman posted to M.T. Section 58th D.A.C. Weather:- mild with periods of rain.	
	16th		2/Lieut H.S. Gilberry posted to 2 T.M.Bty. Lieut K.A.R. Strathman joined from 2/58 T.M.Bty. posted to Section 58th D.A.C. Capt the Rev. A.L. Newton C.F. joined. Weather:- mild & slight frost at night.	
	17th		2 Horses evacuated M.V.S. Debility	
	18th		12 Reinforcements (all Drivers) arrived Weather:- mild. fine.	
	19th		2/Lieut H. Ponsonby arrived.	
	20th		1 man admitted to hospital. 1 man proclaimed from hospital. Weather:- mild.	

AF C2118

WAR DIARY of 56th D.A.C.

Sheet 3

Place	Date	Hour	Summary of Events and Information	Remarks & references to appendices
WARLUCOURT	21st	9/c	No 2 Section moved to BIENVILLERS. 1 mule died exhaustion. Lieut F. Atkinson attached 1 M.R By. 1 man discharged from Hospital. Weakened with sleet and snow. 56th Division transferred to VII Corps.	
	22nd		1 man admitted to Hospital. 1 man discharged from Hospital. 1 man admitted C.C.S. No 20 — struck by lightning. Weather mild. Thaw continues.	
	26th		D.D.V.S. inspects animals 17 Nov. 2 sections Orders received "to be ready to move"	

AF C2118

WAR DIARY

Sheet IV

58th D.A.C.
March 1917

Place	Date	Hour	Summary of Events & Information	Remarks & References to appendices

WARLINCOURT

Horses. Condition of.
As noted in my war diary for February 1917, 156 horses were lent to the Divisional Train. These horses were very emaciated when returned and seemingly neglected. This together with the horses loaned to the R.E.'s and the bad state of the roads pretty nearly account as for the number of animals evacuated during the month.

Meats. Good. a few cases of German measles.

Weather
Generally cold with snow, many nights fros[t]y. During the middle of the month the roads became very bad rendering transport very difficult

[signature]
Lieut. Col. R.F.A.,
Commanding 58th (Lon.) D.A.C.

A.F. C2118

WAR DIARY
58" D.A.C. April 1917.
Summary of Events and Information

Place	Date	Hour	Summary of Events and Information	Remarks & references to appendices
BIENVILLERS	15/4/17	9⁰⁰am	Left BIENVILLERS.	CoP.
ERVILLIERS	15/4/17	3⁰⁰pm	arrived ERVILLIERS.	CoP.

J.P.L. of A. Evans.
Lieut. Col. R.F.A.,
Commanding 58th (Lon.) D.A.C.

Vol 5

CONFIDENTIAL
****

WAR DIARY

OF

56th D.A.C.

From 1/5/17
To 28/5/17

WAR DIARY
INTELLIGENCE SUMMARY.
(Erase heading not required.)

Army Form C. 2118.

Place	Date	Hour	Summary of Events and Information	Remarks and references to Appendices
In the field			NIL	

J. D. Loyd ---
Lieut. Col. R.F.A.,
Commanding 58th (Lon.) D.A.C.

WAR DIARY
INTELLIGENCE SUMMARY
(Erase heading not required.)

Army Form C. 2118.

Place	Date	Hour	Summary of Events and Information	Remarks and references to Appendices
In the Field			58 D.A.C. N/L	

Vol 6

30/6/17

Ernest Fellmy
Lieut. & Adjutant,
58th (London) Divisional Ammunition Column.

SECRET.

WAR DIARY

INTELLIGENCE SUMMARY.
(Erase heading not required.)

58th (London) D.A.C.

Month Ending July 1917.

No. 2850
Army Form C. 2118.

Place	Date	Hour	Summary of Events and Information	Remarks and references to Appendices
In the field	4/7/17		D.A.C. marched from camp at ERVILLERS - BEHAGNIES to "A" Camp, FRICOURT. H.Q. No 2 and 3 Sections to "A" Camp, FRICOURT. No 1 Section accompanied 290 Bde R.F.A. to location near YPRES - Sheet 27c. Arthur 2, V.3.c.4.4.	
In the field	10/7/17		H.Q. No 2 and 3 Sections marched from "A" Camp FRICOURT to Camp at YTRES - LECHELLE. Locations (Sheet 57c Edition 2). H.Q. P 31. d.1.8. No 2 Sec - P.25 d.6.6. No 3 Sec - P.25 d.5.5. No 1 Section did not move.	

Arthur Hoardy. Capt R.A.
Comdg (pro tem) 58th (London) D.A.C.

SECRET

WAR DIARY

58th (London) Divl. Sab. — Week Ending 3/8/17

Vol 8 Page 1.

3274
3 AUG 1917

Summary of Events and Information

Place	Date	Hour		Remarks
	26/8/17		(a) Move of HQ Staff, No 1 Section and No 2 Section.	
			HQ, No 1 Section and No 2 Section marched to ARRAS from locations as under:—	
			HQ Staff } Sheet 51 B. M.17.c.	
			No 1 Section }	
			No 2 Section. Sheet 57 C. A.12.d.7.7.	
	Night of 26-27/8/17		Entrained from ARRAS to POPERINGHE.	
	27/8/17		Marched from POPERINGHE to locations as under:—	
			HQ Staff } Sheet 28. G.26.a.1.9.	
			No 2 Section }	
			No 1 Section. Sheet 28. G.26.d.0.2.	
			(b) Move of No 3 Section	
	27/8/17		Marched to ARRAS from location at M.M.C., Sheet 51 B	
			and entrained to GODEWAERSVELDE.	
	28/8/17		Marched from GODEWAERSVELDE to location at L.36.c.central Sheet 27.	

Page 2

WAR DIARY

58th (London) D.A.C. — Month ending 31/8/17

Place	Date Hour	Summary of Events and Information	Remarks
	30/8/17	D.A.C. moved Complete to locations as under. —	
		H.Q. H. 31. d. 5. 1. Sheet 28	
		No 1 Section. H. 32. c. 5. 7. "	
		No 2 Section. H. 32. a. 7. 4. "	
		No 3 Section. H. 32. c. 7. 8. "	

J. D. Lloyd Evans
Lieut. Col. R.F.A.
Commanding 58th (London) D.A.C.

31/8/17 to Hq. R.A.
55th (London) Division.

SECRET

WAR DIARY

58th (London) D.A.C. – month ending 30/9/17.

Summary of Events and Information

Place	Date	Hour		Remarks

3/9/17   D.A.C. moved complete
from locations as under:—

     HQ.   H.31. d.5.1.   (Sheet 28).
     No.1 Sec: H.32. c. 5.7.   "
     No.2 "   H.32. a. 7.4.   "
     No.3 "   H.32. c. 7.8.   "

to billets at LE NOUVEAU MONDE (near HERZEELE).

7/9/17   D.A.C. moved complete – to relieve 23rd D.A.C. –
from LE NOUVEAU MONDE
to locations as under:—

     HQ   A.30. 6.9.7.   (Sheet 28)
     No.1 Sec.   A. 30. 6.9.9.   (")
     No.2 "   B. 25. a 3.3.   (")
     No.3 "   B. 26. c. 9.2.   (")

(sd) for H.Q.R.A. 58th (Lond) Division   J.D.L. Evans
30/9/17   Lieut. Col. R.F.A.,
     Commanding 58th (Lond) D.A.C.

AF £2118 58

WAR DIARY

58th (London) Divnl Ammn Column

58th (London) Divisional Ammunition Column — No. W.202 — 9 DEC 1917

Place	Date	Hour	Summary of Events and Information	Remarks and references to Appendices
VLAMERTINGHE	2/11/17	7.30 am	The Column marched from camp in VLAMERTINGHE Area to NORMHOUDT Area.	
NORMHOUDT	3/11/17	8 am	The Column marched from NORMHOUDT to RECQUES ARTILLERY Area. HQrs at RUMINGHEM.	
RUMINGHEM	12/11/17	8 am	The Column marched to DESVRES AREA. HQrs at DESVRES.	
DESVRES	13/11/17	8 am	The Column marched to ESTREE ARTILLERY Area. HQrs at TUBERSENT	
TUBERSENT	14/11/17	2 pm	HQrs removed to FRENCQ.	
FRENCQ	18/11/17	1 pm	HQrs removed to MARESVILLE.	

6/12/17.

J.D. Lloyd Evans,
Lieut. Col. R.F.A.
Commanding 58th (Lon) D.A.C.

58th (Lon) Division

WAR DIARY.

58th (London) Divisional Ammunition Column.

HEADQUARTERS 58th (LONDON) D.A.C.
No. 4406
Date 1/1/18

Place	Date.	Hour.	Summary of Events and Information.	Remarks and References to Appendices
MARESVILLE.	4/12/17	8.30 a.m.	The Column marched to THIEMBRONNE Artillery Area, with Headquarters at MERCK-St-LIEVIN.	
MERCK-St-LIEVIN	5/12/17	9 a.m.	The Column marched to LEDERZEELE.	
LEDERZEELE.	6/12/17	9.30 a.m.	The Column marched to ZERMEZEELE.	
ZERMEZEELE	7/12/17	7 a.m.	The Column marched to HAMHOEK Artillery Area, with Headquarters located at "X" Camp, A.16.b.5.2. (Sheet 28 N.W.)	
—	15/12/17	12 noon	Headquarters moved to ROUSSEL FARM Camp, B.13.a.3.7 (Sheet 28 N.W).	

J.D.Lloyd M Evans Lieut. Col. R.A.
Commanding 58th (London) Divnl. Ammun. Col.

To:- H.Q.R.A.
58th (London) Division

1/1/18.

SECRET

Army Form C. 2118.

WAR DIARY
INTELLIGENCE SUMMARY
(Erase heading not required.)

58th (London) D.A.C.
Month ending 31/1/18

Place	Date	Hour	Summary of Events and Information	Remarks and references to Appendices
—	13/1/18	—	Column marched from ROUSSEL FARM Camp B.13.a.3.7 (Sheet 28 NW) to Staging Area as under:— HQ Staff – PARDO Camp F.14.c.8.6. (Sheet 27) No 1 & 2 Sections – E.24.a.9.3 (Sheet 27) Baa Section A.19.b.1.8. (Sheet 28)	
—	27-24/1/18	—	Column marched from Staging Area to PROVEN, then entrained, detrained at VILLERS-BRETONNEUX and marched to Billets at VAIRE	
—	28/1/18	—	Column marched to new locations as under:— HQ Staff and No 2 Section – HERLY No 1 Section – ETALON Baa Section – SEPT-FOURS	
—	29/1/18	—	Column marched to BABŒUF	
—	31/1/18	—	HQ RA 58th (Lon) Div	

F.D. Lloyd Evans
Lieut. Col. R.F.A.
Commanding 58th (Lon) D.A.C.

SECRET

Army Form C. 2118.

WAR DIARY
or
INTELLIGENCE SUMMARY.
(Erase heading not required.)

Instructions regarding War Diaries and Intelligence Summaries are contained in F. S. Regs., Part II. and the Staff Manual respectively. Title pages will be prepared in manuscript.

58th (London) A.C. Month ending 28-2-18.

Place	Date	Hour	Summary of Events and Information	Remarks and references to Appendices
BABOEUF	6-2-18		Column marched to OGNES.	

27-2-18
H.Q. R.A.
58th (Lon) Div.

Arthur F Landy. Capt. R.F.A.
Temp. Comdg. 58th (London) Div.

58th (London) D.A.C.

WAR DIARY – March 1918

Date	Hour	Summary of Events or Information	Remarks
22/3/18	1.P.M	D.A.C. marched from OGNES to new locations as under:— H.Q. and S.A.A Section — BABOEUF No 1 and 2 Sections — MONDESCOURT.	No 1/5
23/3/18	5. P.M	D.A.C. marched, complete, to QUIERZY #	# Here 96th B.a.c (Lt Col) came under Command of OC 58 DAC
24/3/18	1.30 P.M	D.A.C } marched, Complete, to BOURGUIGNON 96th B.A.C }	
25/3/18	1. P.M.	D.A.C } marched to new location as under:— 96th B.A.C } H.Q, No 2 Section, SAA Section and 96th B.A.C. — BLERANCOURT No 1 Section — CUTS	
26/3/18		No 1 Section marched to St PAUL.	
27/3/18	12 noon	D.A.C } marched Complete, to LE MESNIL. 96th B.A.C } (No 1 Section via St AUBIN)	

4 April 1918
H.Q. R.A
58th (Lond) Division

J. D. Ligatrad
Lieut. Col. R.F.A.
Commanding 58th (Lond) D.A.C.

WAR DIARY

58th DIVISIONAL AMMUNITION COLUMN.

A P R I L

1 9 1 8

SECRET

Army Form C. 2118.

58

38th (London) DAC
April 1918

No 106 16

WAR DIARY
INTELLIGENCE SUMMARY
(Erase heading not required)

Place	Date	Hour	Summary of Events and Information	Remarks and references to Appendices
	1-4-18	1pm	D.A.C. and 96th B.A.C. moved from LE MESNIL to following locations:-	
			H.Q. and B.A.C. – CHEVILLE COURT	
			No 1 Sec and S.A.A Section – CHRISTOPHE. A. BERRY	
			No 2 Section – HAUTEBRAYE	
	3-4-18	12.15am	D.A.C. and 96th B.A.C. commenced to march to VILLERS COTTERET and LONGPONT to entrain for SALEUX and LONGEAU; hence D.A.C. marched to locations as under which were occupied by 3.30 p.m. 5/4/18:-	
			H.Q. – CAGNY: No 1 Section – Bd DE St QUENTIN, AMIENS:	
			No 2 Section – RUE DE CAGNY, BOUTILLERIE: S.A.A Section – Iron foundry, BOUTILLERIE.	
	7-4-18	2pm	D.A.C. less S.A.A Section marched to locations near GUSY, with HQ at N.26.a.9.9 (Sheet 62.D) to relieve 16th DAC — on relief, coming under orders of 5th Australian D.A.	
			Notification received – 58th HQ RA memo ADA 146 d/5-4-18 that SAA Section controlled by 58th Div "Q".	
	11-4-18	2pm	DAC less SAA Section marched to locations near LAMOTTE (N. of SOMME R)	
			(with HQ at N.8.d.3.2 (Sheet 62.D)	

SECRET

Army Form C. 2118.

WAR DIARY
INTELLIGENCE SUMMARY. 58th (London) D.A.C. — May, 1918
(Erase heading not required.)

Vol 17

Place	Date	Hour	Summary of Events and Information	Remarks and references to Appendices
EAUCOURT SUR SOMME	4/5/18	9 am	S.A.A. Section. 58 DAC marched from EAUCOURT-SUR-SOMME and joined 173rd Infy Bde Transport Column at BOURDON	
BOURDON	7/5/18	8.30 am	S.A.A. Section marched from BOURDON to present location near CONTAY. C.3. central (Sheet 62 D)	
EAUCOURT SUR SOMME	16/5/18	9 am	HQ., Section 1 and Section 2, 58 DAC marched from EAUCOURT-SUR-SOMME and entered Billets at BELLOY	
BELLOY	17/5/18	6.30 am	HQ., Section 1 and Section 2, 58 DAC marched from BELLOY to present locations as under :— HQ. — CONTAY. Billet No 24. No1 Section — B.6.d.15 (Sheet-62.D). near BEAUCOURT. No2 " — T.29.C.6.2 (Sheet 57D).	
CONTAY	24/5/18		Major C. HARRIS (DO) RA assumed Command of 58th DAC vice Lt-Col J.D. Lloyd-Evans R.F.A. (to England) 24/5/18.	
1/6/18	H.Q R.A. 58th (Lond.) Divn			

O. Harris Major (DO) RA
Condg. 58th (London) DAC

Secret

58th (London) D.A.C
Month ending 30 June 1918

Army Form C. 2118.

WAR DIARY
INTELLIGENCE SUMMARY.
(Erase heading not required.)

Instructions regarding War Diaries and Intelligence Summaries are contained in F. S. Regs., Part II. and the Staff Manual respectively. Title pages will be prepared in manuscript.

Place	Date	Hour	Summary of Events and Information	Remarks and references to Appendices
				98/19
CONTAY	8/6/18	9 am	S.A.A. Section marched from CONTAY to B.q.c. – (Sheet 62.D) and passed under orders of "Q", 58th Div. near MOLLIENS-AU-BOIS	
CONTAY	9/6/18	10.30 am	D.A.C., less S.A.A Section marched from CONTAY and entered billets at LONGPRÉ	
B.q.c.	10/6/18	8.30 am	S.A.A. Section marched to PICQUIGNY.	
LONGPRÉ	10/6/18	6.15 am	D.A.C. less S.A.A. Section marched from LONGPRÉ and entered billets at BEHENCOURT with Headquarters at the Chateau.	
PICQUIGNY	20/6/18	7.30 am	S.A.A Section marched (still under orders of "Q") from PICQUIGNY to C3 central – (Sheet 62.D) near CONTAY.	
	24/6/18	noon	S.A.A. Came under orders of O.C. 58th DAC	
30/6/18	HQ. R.A. 58th (London)			

MAJOR, (D.O.) R.A.
COMDG. 58TH (L) D.A.C.

SECRET

WAR DIARY
INTELLIGENCE SUMMARY.
(Erase heading not required.)

Army Form C. 2118.

58th (London) Div. Month ending 31st July 1918

Place	Date	Hour	Summary of Events and Information	Remarks and references to Appendices
H.Q. R.A. 58th (London) Div.	31/7/18		NIL RETURN	

J Davis
MAJOR, (D.O.) R.A.
COMDG. 58TH (L) D.A.O.

58th Divl. Artillery

58th DIVISIONAL AMMUNITION COLUMN,

AUGUST 1918.

SECRET.

WAR DIARY
or
INTELLIGENCE SUMMARY.
(Erase heading not required.)

58th (London) Bal
Month ending 31/8/18

Army Form C. 2118.

VR 20

Place	Date	Hour	Summary of Events and Information	Remarks and references to Appendices
near CONTAY	3/8/18	8.00am	Lan Section moved from C.3. Central, near CONTAY (Sheet 62 D)	
			to QUERRIEU and came under orders of "Q", 58th (Lond) Divn	
BEHENCOURT	5/8/18	10.20am	Bal less Lan section moved to LA NEUVILLE (SOMME) – Sheet 62 D.	
LA NEUVILLE	9/8/18	2.30pm	" " " to location I.23.d.central, near BONNAY Sheet 62 D	
BONNAY	12/8/18	9am	" " " to location J.34.b.5.3, near SAILLY-le-SEC Sheet 62 D	
SAILLY-le-SEC	24/8/18	8.30am	" " " to location E.18.central near MEAULTE Sheet 62 D	
MEAULTE	28/8/18	8.30am	" " " to location K.24.a.6.3 near ETINEHEM Sheet 62 D	
ETINEHEM	30/8/18	8. am	" " " to location A.28.b.7.5. near MARICOURT Sheet 62 C.	
31/8/18	HQ Ra 58th (Lond) Division			

signature
MAJOR, (D.C.) R.A.
COMDG. 58TH (L) D.A.O.

17 SECRET

Army Form C. 2118.

WAR DIARY
of
INTELLIGENCE SUMMARY.
(Erase heading not required.)

58th (London) Bab. 7082
Month ending 30th September 1918

Place	Date	Hour	Summary of Events and Information	Remarks and references to Appendices
nr MARICOURT	5/9/18	6.30pm	D.A.C. less 1aa section moved from A28.6.7.5 (Sheet 62.C) near MARICOURT, to location near CLERY-sur-SOMME with HQ. at H6.d.8.0 (Sheet 62.c)	
CLERY s.SOMME	6/9/18	1.30pm	D.A.C., less 1aa section moved to near ALLAINES with HQ at I3.d.cent (" ")	
ALLAINES	9/9/18	9am	D.A.C. less 1aa section moved to near MOISLAINS with HQ at D.2.cent (" ")	
			Note. 1aa section still under orders of "Q". 58th Division	
	30/9/18			

Std. Ra. 58K(Lond.)Aux.

[signature]
MAJOR. (D.O.) R.A.
COMDG. 58TH (L) D.A.C.

SECRET.

WAR DIARY
of
INTELLIGENCE SUMMARY.
(Erase heading not required.)

58th (London) R.A.G.
Month ending 31st October 1918.

Army Form C. 2118.

Place	Date	Hour	Summary of Events and Information	Remarks and references to Appendices
nr. MOISLAINS	8/10/18	0830	D.A.G. (less 1 A/Section) moved from nr. MOISLAINS (D.2. cent. Sheet 62B) to location nr. BONY (Sheet 62B).	9/8 22
nr. BONY	9/10/18	1100	D.A.G. (less 1 A/Section) moved from nr. BONY (Sheet 62B) to location nr. DRENCOURT (Sheet 62c).	
nr. DRENCOURT	10/10/18	1000	D.A.G. (less 1 A/Section) commenced to withdraw from PERONNE and TINCOURT to form First Army.	
	12/10/18		Battalment completed and locations occupied as under :-	
BULLY GRENAY	13/10/18	1100	HQrs. BULLY GRENAY. No. 1 Section. HERSIN. No. 2 Section MOROC.	Sheet 11 (LENS)
MOROC	"	0930	No. 2 Section moved to HERSIN.	
HERSIN	16/10	1130	HQrs moved to HERSIN.	
MONTIGNY	19/10	1130	R.A.G. (less 1 A/Section) moved to Ferme du BARLET, nr. MONTIGNY.	(Sheet 44A)
EVIN	20/10	1030	ditto to EVIN-MALMAISON.	do.
LA VACQUERIE	21/10	0930	ditto to LA VACQUERIE.	do.
			ditto to LANNAY	Sheet 44.
			Note. 1 A/A Section still under orders of 58th Bde "Q"	

C. Harris
MAJOR, (D.O.) R.A.
COMDG. 58TH (L) R.A.G.

58th (London) D.A.C. R.F.A.

WAR DIARY
or
INTELLIGENCE SUMMARY.

Army Form C. 2118.

(Erase heading not required.)

No 2

Place	Date	Hour	Summary of Events and Information	Remarks and references to Appendices
LANNAY	9/11/18	1400	Column (head a section) moved to location near RONCY I.11.c. cent. (Sheet	
nr RONCY	10/11/18	1030	Column (less 1 a.a section) moved to LE CROIX nr NIERS K.3.d. (Sheet 44)	
LE CROIX	11/11/18	0930	Column (less 1 a.a section) moved to GRANDGLISE H.6.c. (Sheet 45)	
S. AMBRUGE	12/11/18	0900	1 a.a section moved to GRANDGLISE and came under orders of O.C. 58th (London) D.A.C.	
			to - MORA 58th (London) D.A.C.	

Signature

MAJOR, (D.O.) R.A.
COMDG. 58TH (L) D.A.C.

58th (London) D.A.C

Army Form C. 2118.

WAR DIARY
or
INTELLIGENCE SUMMARY.
(Erase heading not required.)

Place	Date	Hour	Summary of Events and Information	Remarks and references to Appendices
GRANDGLISE	11/12/18	—	Major C. Harris M.C. R.C.M. (B.O.R.A) proceeded on leave to U.K.—	
do	11/12/18	—	Captain W. Touke M.O., R.F.A., assumed temporary command during the absence of Major C. Harris.	

3/1/19
2o: - H.Q.R.A.,
58th (London) Division -

J.W.Touke Capt. R.F.A.
Temp. Comdg. 58th (London) D.A.C.

WAR DIARY
or
INTELLIGENCE SUMMARY. 58 Div

(Erase heading not required.)

Place	Date	Hour	Summary of Events and Information	Remarks and references to Appendices
			58th (London) D.A.C., R.F.A.	
			Nothing to record during April, 1919.	
To. H.Q. 58th Div. front.	1-5-19			

H.V. Monype Capt.,
R.F.A.,
Commanding 58th (Lon.) D.A.C.

WAR DIARY
INTELLIGENCE SUMMARY.
(Erase heading not required.)

Army Form C. 2118.

Place	Date	Hour	Summary of Events and Information	Remarks and references to Appendices
BELGIUM	1 to 31/5/19		58th (London) D.A.	
			Nothing to report during the month	
	31/5/19		To: HQ. 58th Divis: Arnt.	

H.W. Moule Capt.
R.F.A.
Commanding 58th (Lond.) D.A.C.

www.ingramcontent.com/pod-product-compliance
Lightning Source LLC
Chambersburg PA
CBHW081458160426

43193CB00013B/2526